He Just *THINKS* He's Not That Into You

The *Insanely* Determined Girl's Guide to Getting the Man She Wants

He Just _THINKS_ He's Not That Into You

The _Insanely_ Determined Girl's Guide to Getting the Man She Wants

By Danielle Whitman

RUNNING PRESS

PHILADELPHIA • LONDON

9 8 7 6 5 4 3 2 1
Digit on the right indicates the number of this printing

Library of Congress Control Number: 2006934559

ISBN-13: 978-0-7624-2964-6
ISBN-10: 0-7624-2964-X

Cover and interior illustrations by Chuck Gonzales
Cover and interior design by Melissa Gerber
Typography: Adobe Garamond, Goudy, Archies Hand, Alexs Hand, Bell MT, EdPS Bengbats, EdPS Script, EdPS Brush, EdPS Roman, Secret Recipe, Coquette Bold, and Wendy.

This book may be ordered by mail from the publisher. Please include $2.50 for postage and handling.
But try your bookstore first!

Running Press Book Publishers
2300 Chestnut Street, Suite 200
Philadelphia, Pennsylvania 19103-4399

Visit us on the web!
www.runningpress.com

Dedication

For my darling Trevor

It took forever to find you.
But thanks to that bracelet
on your ankle, next time
it'll be a snap.

♥   ♥   ♥   ♥   ♥   ♥   ♥   ♥   ♥   ♥   ♥   ♥   ♥   ♥

Introduction

He Just Thinks *He's Not That Into You* is built on a basic principle: Men don't know what they want. So it's up to you, the strong, loving, forceful women of the world, to show them.

Some of you are looking for love, some of you are already involved. And some of you have been court-ordered to keep your distance. But whatever the circumstance, if the man of your dreams isn't returning your affection, you cannot take it personally. You have to remember, it's not you, it's him. Let's face it, most men are cowards. Afraid to love, afraid to commit, afraid of you.

It's ironic that men often refer to the women in their lives as "the old ball and chain," but the second you so much as handcuff them to a radiator, they start screaming about legal rights, false imprisonment, "I can't feel my fingers!", blah, blah, blah.

This guide is meant to empower you and inspire you. It's culled from letters from women just like you, all over the country. You will read about real-life situations that I'm sure you can all relate to. I'll also offer helpful tips and inspirational thoughts to send you down the path to true love.

Remember, the insanely determined girl does not take "No" for an answer. She sees "No" as an invitation, an opportunity. She knows that you can't spell "matrimony" without an "N" and an "O."

Getting to Know Him
A Stranger Is Just a Husband You Haven't Met Yet

You've spotted that special someone. You feel an instant connection. Yet you're unsure about his feelings. Well, let's face it, a woman knows when she's met "the one" long before a man does, so it's not uncommon for a woman to have to do more of the work in the beginning of a relationship. But it'll pay off big time when the man of your schemes becomes the man of your dreams!

• •

Q. I have been going to the same grocery store for years. There is a very cute bag boy who always flirts with me, but he never asks me out. I know he wants to because he always says "have a nice day", and he doesn't say it to everybody. I think he doesn't want to ask me out because he's embarrassed that he's just a bag boy.

• •

A. If he wasn't interested, he'd simply say, "Thank you." And by saying, "Have a nice day," he's of course implying, "with me." He's offering to show you a nice time. Time to take the hint (he's practically hitting you over the head!), grab the bag by the handles, and take home that in-store special! Soon the grocery aisle won't be the only aisle you'll be walking down!

Q. I met this guy at a bar and we really hit it off. He took my number, and then didn't call me. Do you think he's just not that into me?

P.S. He wouldn't give me his number. Or his name.

● ●

A. Why would a man take your number, say he's going to call, and then not call? Something doesn't add up! And you owe it to both of you to find out what's happened. There must be evidence left at the bar—his DNA, a hair sample. Or is there anything of yours he might have touched that you can have dusted for fingerprints? Cigarette lighter? Pen? Breast? Good luck!

● ●

Reasons a Guy Doesn't Call after You've Given him your Number

- ❤ He lost it.

- ❤ His dog ate it.

- ❤ He washed his jeans with your number in the pocket and now it's all smeared.

- ❤ He's scared because the chemistry between you was so intense.

- ❤ His phone is broken.

- ❤ Your phone is broken.

- ❤ He's been injured in an accident.

- He's been killed.

- He's just trying to figure out how to get out of another relationship so he can be with you.

- He's incredibly busy at work and doesn't want to call until he has the time to give you his full attention.

- He was struck on the head and is wandering the streets with amnesia, only remembering your name and that he loves you.

. . . .

Q. There's a guy I see jogging all the time in my neighborhood. I try to strike up conversations with him, but I can never get his attention. It's like he doesn't hear me calling, or see me running after him or anything. One time I almost caught up to him in my car, but he obviously didn't see me because he cut through someone's yard and I couldn't follow. I really want to meet him!

. . . .

A. He probably doesn't hear you because he's wearing an iPod or there's a lot of traffic noise. Either way, the idea is not to start from behind. You know where he's going—be there ahead of him. Perhaps offer him an ice-cold beverage, or some homemade cookies, or an Olympic torch made out of tin foil. Something that will start a conversation. You're obviously on the right "track"! All men are runners at first. You just have to teach them to run *toward* you instead of away!

Useful Tip

A sure way to a man's heart is to get to know his dog. Take it for a long walk. Spend a few days with it (rope can be chewed through, chain can't). At the very least, he'll come looking for it.

Q. I met a really cool guy at a party. We totally hit it off. At the end of the night, he wouldn't give me his phone number, but he gave me his e-mail address. I've e-mailed him a bunch of times, but he never e-mails back. Now when I e-mail him, it comes back as blocked spam. Do you think he's changed his mind about me?

A. He wouldn't have given you his e-mail address if he wasn't interested. As to being blocked . . . His computer could have a virus. He could have accidentally blocked you by hitting a bad key stroke. Or he could just be out of town—you should find out where he lives from the host of the party and go over and find out.

Why Men Don't Ask You Out

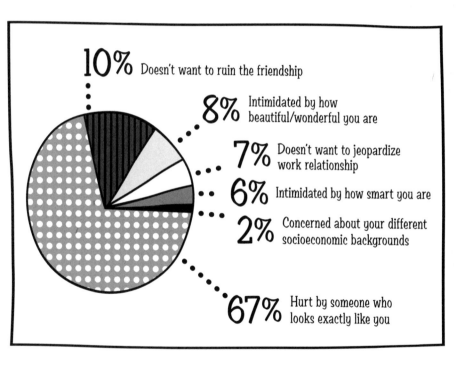

10% Doesn't want to ruin the friendship

8% Intimidated by how beautiful/wonderful you are

7% Doesn't want to jeopardize work relationship

6% Intimidated by how smart you are

2% Concerned about your different socioeconomic backgrounds

67% Hurt by someone who looks exactly like you

Useful Tip:

Information is king. If you learn a man's habits, you can use them to your advantage. Follow him around, find out where he goes, what he likes. If you know he likes to get coffee in the morning, get a job at Starbucks. Then when he walks in for his morning fix, you can say, "Double decaf latte, extra foam." He'll appreciate the effort you took to learn about him!

Love in the Workplace

Forbidden? Or for You?

A lot of employers frown on work romances because they fear that if the relationship breaks up, it can cause tension in the workplace. But that's never going to happen. Why would you end a relationship when it was fate that led you and your man to work together? Fate . . . or a private detective!

Workplace romances give you a chance to be with the guy you love twenty-four seven. And who wouldn't want that? It's also a great opportunity to keep your eye on your guy once you've made him yours. Because as we all know, there are a lot of desperate women out there in the workplace looking to snag a man.

Q. I asked out my co-worker. He said no and made up this story that he was living with his girlfriend, (I know he isn't because I broke into his apartment when was away on a business trip and NO WOMAN LIVES THERE!) Why would he lie to me?

A. First of all, congratulations on taking the initiative and doing your research. Clearly you have read my column, "The Fire Escape: Not Just an Exit."

Now, onto your problem. Obviously the work situation is holding him back. If he's your superior, he's afraid of a sexual harassment suit if it doesn't work out. If he's your subordinate, he's intimidated by you. If you're on an equal level, he's afraid of the pain of seeing you every day at the office after you no longer love him. Let him know this will never be the case. You will always love him. The truth is, relationships at the office are tricky. The easiest solution is to get him fired. He might be a little upset at first, but then he'll realize it was worth it. Besides, it's a tough job market out there. When he has nowhere to turn, where's he going to run but into your loving arms?

How to Get a Co-Worker Fired so You Can Date Him

- ❤ Steal office supplies. Put office supplies in co-worker's drawer. Call in anonymous tip.

- ❤ Buy drugs. Plant drugs in co-worker's desk. Call in anonymous tip.

- ❤ Write perverted e-mails. Send from co-worker's computer.

- ❤ Tape record co-worker. Edit tape to make obscene message. Leave on boss's voice mail.

- ❤ Send flowers and gifts to yourself. Sign them from co-worker. File sexual harassment suit against co-worker.

- ❤ Drug co-worker's coffee. Wait until co-worker passes out. Report to boss that co-worker is sleeping on the job.

- ❤ Drug co-worker's coffee. Wait until co-worker passes out. Undress co-worker and leave in boss's office naked.

Q. There's this guy at work that I like. After I asked him to go out with me like ten times, he finally agreed (I think he was just scared because we work together). We ended up having sex. Now we have sex all the time, but he always leaves right away afterward. We never go out on dates or go anywhere. Do you think I'm just a booty call?

. . . .

A. First of all, there's nothing wrong with being "just a booty call." The way to a man's heart is not through his stomach. *Wink, wink!* Seems to me this relationship is heading in the right direction—there's no way you can have repeated sexual encounters with a man without his heart ultimately opening to you. And as for him never taking you out in public, perhaps he's afraid of being spotted by a co-worker who'll try to put a stop to the romance. Or maybe it's simply that he's saving money on dinners and trivial entertainment so that he can spend it on a ring! Send me an invite!

. . . .

Q. This guy at work turned down several of my invitations to go on a date. When I insisted on knowing why, he finally said it was because I was overweight. I weigh 430 pounds. I think he's actually really attracted to me, but doesn't want other people to know he's a chubby chaser. Or he's letting his friends influence his thinking.

A. The fact that he told you you're too heavy means that he's willing to enter into honest and open meaningful dialogue with you, something lacking in many relationships. It's also clear that he's been checking you out. You're not just another invisible co-worker. And by commenting on your body, he's even willing to risk a sexual harassment suit. Sounds like true love to me! So don't let his friends decide where this relationship is going. You're bigger than them.

Boyfriend Problems

Please. If You Have a Boyfriend, What's the Problem?

So congratulations, you've gotten your man! It's unrealistic not to expect a few little bumps along the road to matrimony. But don't make mountains out of those molehills! Stay the course. He wouldn't have become your boyfriend if you weren't destined to spend the rest of your lives together.

Q. I have a boyfriend (although he doesn't like me using that term). We have a great sex life, although often (usually) he leaves me "unsatisfied." He doesn't seem to care, but just gets up and watches TV or something. What does this mean? I really love him!

A. Sounds like he loves you too. Because despite your being so obviously hard to please, he's sticking with you. Sure, he may leave you unsatisfied, but he doesn't leave. And you know what they say, "If it ain't broke, don't fix it." Just keep doing what you're doing!

Q. I've been dating Phil a long time, and we're really in love. But whenever I bring up marriage, he changes the subject and sometimes even disappears for days after. What should I do?

. . . .

A. Sounds like you've got yourself a shy one! The truth is, sometimes guys just need a little push. I'm sure you've seen those reality shows where they surprise someone on the street with a fun makeover. What about a surprise wedding? He sounds like the perfect candidate. You whisk him into a limo. Have a tuxedo ready. Have all his friends and family waiting. He'll be so excited he'll barely be able to squeak out "I do!" Then it's back into the limo, and the two of you will be driving off to a wonderful future together.

. . . .

Relationship Stages to Celebrate!

- ❤ One-week anniversary
- ❤ Two-week anniversary
- ❤ Three-week anniversary
- ❤ Four-week anniversary
- ❤ One-month anniversary (no, they are *not* the same!)
- ❤ Five-week anniversary
- ❤ Etc.

Q. My boyfriend travels a lot and doesn't ever call me from the road. Should I read anything into this?

• •

A. Absolutely! You should read into it that some states have very poor cell phone reception. And some places (Amish country, for example) have no phones at all. And even if there are phones in the hotel, their long-distance charges are astronomical. He's obviously trying to save money to spend on the two of you. Maybe he's saving for a ring!

• •

Q. My boyfriend never says, "I love you" even though I say it to him <u>all the time</u>. And then he'll reply, "Thank you," or "That's cool." He won't even say, "Ditto." I know he does love me, it's just not that easy for him to express deep emotions. How can I get him to open up?

● ●

A. He wouldn't be "cool" with you loving him if he didn't feel the same way. You just have to make him feel safe enough to share his feelings. The police have a technique to get people to open up to them. It's called "good cop, bad cop." And while it usually works best with two people, there's no reason you alone can't play both roles. The "bad/unpredictable/scary" cop will soon have him running into the arms of "good/understanding/protective" cop. Then before you know it, you'll be calling in a 10-24. That's police talk for "assignment complete!"

● ●

Songs to Live By . . . and Love By

- ❤ "Every Breath You Take," Sting

- ❤ "Can't Live (If Living Is Without You)," Harry Nilsson

- ❤ "White Flag," Dido

- ❤ "You Oughta Know," Alanis Morrisette

- ❤ "How Do I Live," LeAnn Rimes

- ❤ "Ain't Too Proud to Beg," The Temptations

Q. I've been seeing this guy, and I thought things were going really well. Until he told me that he thinks I'm "scary psycho" and that he doesn't want anything to do with me. I really love him and I don't want to lose him. What should I do?

P.S. I admit that "seeing him" means through his kitchen window.

A. There are many definitions of a relationship, and it's up to you to set the parameters, not him. Perhaps you should show him what "scary psycho" really is. There's a big difference between showing up in someone's shower with a butcher knife (more trouble than it's worth!) and waiting patiently outside at all hours of the day and night. Demonstrate that you're the only one who will always be there for him!

Suspicious Minds

It's Only a Problem if You Think It Is

I get a lot of letters from women questioning the behavior of their men. He's keeping odd hours, he's not coming home, there must be something wrong with the relationship. Well, it's that kind of suspicious attitude that drives men away. And if you're going to be driving anywhere with a man, it should be in a stretch limo with the words "Just Married" on the back!

Q. I got stood up on a date. The guy said he was in a car accident and broke his back. But then I saw him a week later with a blonde girl Roller-Blading. Do you think he lied to me?

A.   Why are women so negative? He was probably just thanking his sister or the nurse who helped him recuperate. Some people heal very quickly. It sounds miraculous, but perhaps it was the thought of you that kept him going and made him able to walk again. This is true love. Don't let it skate by you.

Q. I had sex with a guy I didn't know on an airplane (great sex by the way!). He said he'd call me the next morning and then he didn't. What happened? Do you think he was just using me to join the "Mile High Club"?

A. No. Many a great romance has started this way. Don't you watch television or the movies? You could not have had great sex unless he really cared about you. Maybe something's wrong with your phone. Call the phone company to see if your phone went out (more common than you think). If your phone is working, you need to go to his house and check his phone. Get a hold of the passenger list and get his address. While in his house, you'll be able to learn a lot about him—where he works, who his friends are, where he hangs out. With a little initiative, you should be able to get this relationship off the ground and flying high again!

Don't Be a Negative Nelly

- "Please stop calling me" means "I want to see you in person."

- "Leave me alone" means "I want you to be surprised when you see the gift I got you."

- "I never want to see you again" means "until the ceremony, or it's bad luck."

- "I'm seeing someone" means "I'm seeing a therapist 'cause I'm crazy in love with you."

- "Stop following me" means "I want you by my side!"

- "I'm calling the police" means "to arrest you for stealing my heart!"

- "I can't breathe" means "You take my breath away."

- "Stop telling everyone I'm your boyfriend" means "Start telling them I'm your husband!"

Q. My boyfriend is terrific, and I feel petty complaining. But every time we go out, I'm the one who pays. I also pay for his clothes, his living expenses, and recently he asked me for a Porsche. Which I had no problem buying because I love him, I have a lot of money, and I love seeing him happy. He's very appreciative, but seems to have no ambition or desire to get a job (although he did say he'd love to start a band if I wanted to sponsor him). Lately he doesn't even seem to have in interest in sex, which is weird because I found a receipt for a large amount of condoms charged to my credit card. Do you think that the relationship is in trouble? He's always said he loves me and that our age difference doesn't bother him (I'm 63; he's 27).

• •

A. Stop looking for problems where there are none. You say he has no ambition, yet he's willing to put in the time and effort to become a rock and roll star so that *he* can support *you*. And why would he want a boring nine-to-five job when that would take him away from you from nine to five? He obviously adores you. He knows buying him things makes you happy, and your happiness is the most important thing to him. As for the condoms, he's probably saving them for the honeymoon, so make sure you take him somewhere nice!

• •

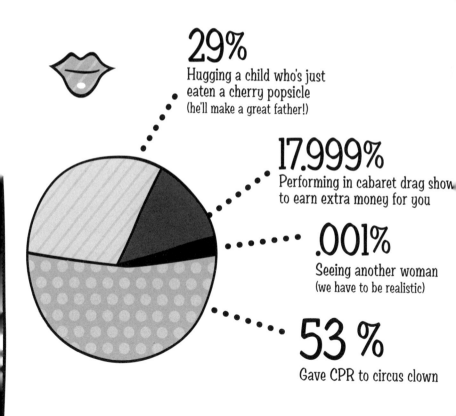

29%
Hugging a child who's just
eaten a cherry popsicle
(he'll make a great father!)

17.999%
Performing in cabaret drag show
to earn extra money for you

.001%
Seeing another woman
(we have to be realistic)

53 %
Gave CPR to circus clown

Q. My boyfriend went on a business trip. Even though he told me never to call his hotel room, even in an emergency, after repeated unreturned calls to his cell phone, I called the hotel. A woman answered in his room. Do you think he's cheating on me?

. . . .

A. Don't be such a drama queen. There are plenty of explanations for a strange woman in your man's hotel room late at night. Maid service, room service, a business meeting that went late, or maybe he simply changed rooms and forgot to tell you. (And why should he? You weren't supposed to call him there!) It's also possible that there was a suicidal woman on the ledge of his window. Your compassionate boyfriend calmed her down and talked her back in. Cut the poor man some slack. And when he comes home from working hard, treat him like the hero he is.

. . . .

Useful Tip

The best way to convince your suspicious mind that there's no one else in your man's life is to cut him off from anyone or anything else he loves—friends, family, work, etc.—leaving him free to spend every waking hour with you!

Getting Him Back
Once You Have Found Him, Never Let Him Go

Okay, so he thinks he wants out. Don't take it personally, it's just biology. From the time of cavemen, men were taught to be hunters. They always think there's something new, something better, waiting around the corner. You need to show your man that the only thing waiting around the corner . . . is *you*. Remember, it takes two people to make a relationship, and it takes two to end it!

Q. We've had four wonderful dates and suddenly my guy broke it off. He tells me he doesn't see a future with me.

A. Four dates isn't enough time to get to know you. If he can't "see a future" with you in it, you need to help him picture it. Be creative. Have a jigsaw puzzle made up with your picture on it, or you and him together. Have address labels made with both of your names so that he can think about your relationship in concrete terms. Call his answering machine and change his outgoing message, "Laurie and David aren't here! They're off throwing Frisbees in the park or taking a moonlit carriage ride or doing other things that people crazy in love like to do. Leave a message!" Soon he'll be leaving you a message: "Come back to me!"

Useful Tip

A good way to hang on to a man is to tell him you're pregnant, even if you're not. Or get pregnant with someone else's baby. Even with intrusive DNA testing, it will still take months for him to find out it's not his baby. Or that there never was a baby. But that's nine months that he's gotten to know you and love you.

● ●

Q. I was seeing this guy for a couple of months, and suddenly he moved with no forwarding address, he changed his phone number, and he switched jobs. Do you think he's trying to avoid me?

● ●

● ●

A. Silly girl. He obviously loves the thrill of the chase, but wants you to do the chasing. If you don't, he'll think you're not that into him. Why are there endless books on how women should play hard to get (ridiculous!), but the minute a man does it, it's considered evasive? Happiness is hiding just out of sight. It's up to you to track it down and flush it out into the open!

● ●

Just Because He's Broken Up with You

- Don't forget his birthday.

- Don't stop having sex with him.

- Don't stop going by his house/calling him/e-mailing him.

- Don't stop asking all of his friends about him.

- Don't lose touch with his family.

- Don't stop doodling his name and yours inside little hearts.

- Don't stop planning that wedding!

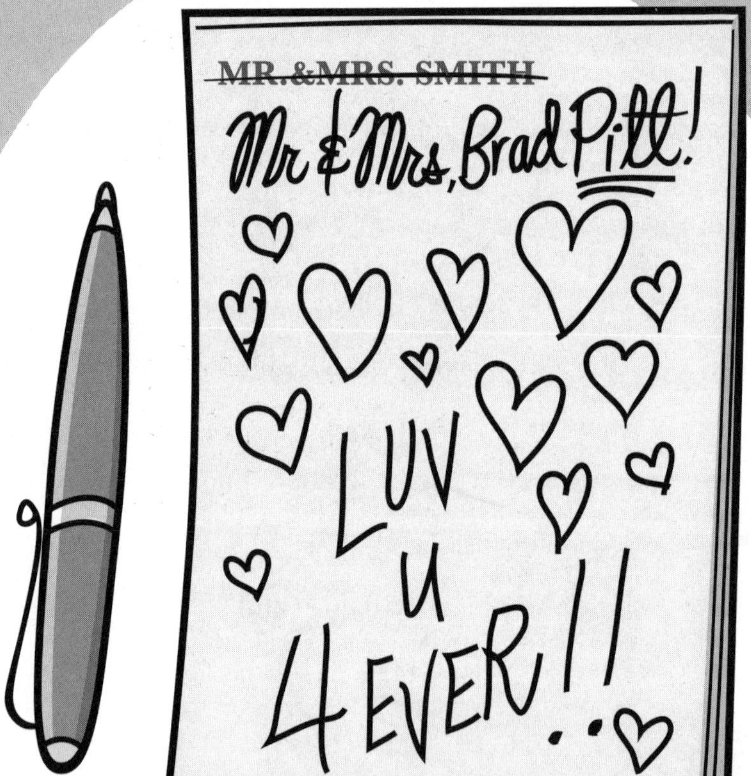
MR.&MRS. SMITH
Mr & Mrs. Brad Pitt!
LUV
U
4 EVER!!

Q. He says he hates me and doesn't ever want to see me again, and he's taken out a restraining order. Help!

●●●●●●●●●●●●●●●●●●●●●●●●●●●●●●●●●●●●●●●

A. This brings to mind a quote from Shakespeare: "Me thinks he doth protest too much." The Bard also wrote, "The course of true love never did run smooth." Sound familiar? And remember, "There's a thin line between love and hate." He just needs that little push toward love. And by the way, if he went to all that trouble to get a restraining order, it's only because he knows he can't restrain *himself!*

●●●●●●●●●●●●●●●●●●●●●●●●●●●●●●●●●●●●●●●

Six Things to Do with a Restraining Order

- ♥ Write love poems on the back and send it to your intended.

- ♥ Use it as a placemat when serving him dinner at his place.

- ♥ Make it into a beautiful origami heart.

- ♥ Use it to wipe off fingerprints.

- ♥ Slide restraining order under locked door. Put hairpin into lock, jiggle until key on other side falls to floor. Slide restraining order out.

- ♥ Shred it into confetti, because you'll need it for the wedding!

Q. I've been dating this guy for about six months and it was going really well. Now he tells me that he wants to break up with me, that it's just not working out and he's met someone else. I know that when he was six years old, he had a puppy and it died. Now I think he's just afraid to love me in case something happens to me like what happened to his puppy. He loves me so much that he'd rather break up with me than lose me.

- -

A. You're very astute. Obviously you've been reading my columns. You have to show him that loss isn't related to love. You can lose things you don't have any attachment to. Take a little caterpillar to his house. Talk about how it lives in its little cocoon, safe from the world, but when it bravely emerges, it's a beautiful, free-flying butterfly, enjoying everything the world has to offer. Then crush it under your shoe. Show him that nothing in life is safe and that death could come at any time. He needs to live for the moment. Good luck!

- -

How to Let a Guy Know You Still Love Him

- ❤ Leave long, detailed messages on his answering machine. (Most machines will record at least thirty minutes of incoming messages.)

- ❤ Hang out at his work, home, gym, favorite stores.

- ❤ Leave love letters and poems on his windshield, in his mailbox, in his locker, at his rebound girlfriend's house.

- ❤ Send him a photo collage of all your happy times together.

- ❤ Drop by with expensive presents.

- ❤ Have his astrological chart done to show him you're soul mates.

- ❤ Make him a popsicle stick diorama depicting your past and your future.

More Songs to Live By

- "Time Is On My Side," Rolling Stones

- "Run For Your Life," The Beatles

- "Crush," Garbage

- "Invisible," Clay Aiken

- "My Bloody Valentine," Good Charlotte

- "The More You Ignore Me (The Closer I Get)," Morrissey

Success Story!

I took your advice and faked a suicide attempt (Twenty-five pills = dead. Twenty-two pills = bad tummy ache). My guy freaked out and left, but I ended up meeting a very cute doctor. We're well on our way to living happily ever after. Actually, I think he's afraid to ask me out because of the whole therapist/patient thing. But I'm not going to let that stop me!

Love Conquers All

Just Because Someone's Not Perfect Doesn't Mean He's Not Perfect for You!

If you look up the definition of taboo, you will find that it means "an inhibition or ban resulting from social custom or emotional aversion." Well, whose emotions count more? Society's? Or your heart's? I think we all know the answer. Forget the naysayers, follow your heart, and you will soon find your wedding on the "Society" page!

Q. My best friend is a guy who I've known forever. I started to have romantic feelings for him and finally confessed that I wanted to take the relationship further. He told me that he couldn't because he thinks he's gay. Admittedly, I've never known him to have a girlfriend, and we love to go shopping together and get mani-pedis, but I thought he was just being a good sport. I think I'm in love with him. Help!

• •

A. The fact that he only "thinks" he's gay is a big sign that he's not gay. If he was gay, he'd know it. Obviously he's attracted to an aggressive, more assertive type of person, and you have to show him that that's you. Take charge! Make him have sex with you!

• •

Q. I like my priest. He says he's not allowed to date and is married to Jesus. Does this mean he's gay? Do you think he's using the vow of celibacy as an excuse?

A. Of course. Confess lots of sexy sins and try to make him hot. Or join a convent. There's a history of relationships between nuns and priests, and also nuns and nuns, so even if you strike out with him, you'll still have a chance at love.

Useful Tip

I had a friend whose husband worked really hard and never took vacations. One day she surprised him by kidnapping him from work and whisking him away for a trip to the Bahamas. He was thrilled, and it only improved their relationship. But there's no reason you should be married, or even in a relationship, to make a thoughtful, romantic gesture.

Q. I really love Daniel, but he says he doesn't want to date me because we're brother and sister. Do you think he's only using this as an excuse?

P.S. He's only my half brother.

A. Some portions of society frown upon siblings marrying, so he's probably afraid of what people will think. He needs to understand that other people's prejudices shouldn't ruin your chance at happiness. Point out all the positives of your union: So many people marry someone they hardly know, while you two have been together your whole lives. You won't have to change your last name. No arguments over where to spend Christmas or Thanksgiving. No fighting over in-laws. And when it comes time to have kids, statistics show that inbred babies grow up to be much happier than most "normal" children.

Motivational Films

- ❤ *The Thorn Birds*

- ❤ *Chinatown*

- ❤ *Mandingo*

- ❤ *Harold and Maude*

- ❤ *Lolita*

- ❤ *National Velvet*

Q. I really like this guy in one of my classes. He's smart, funny, and we have a soul connection for sure. But I think he's a little shy because he's never had a real girlfriend before. He keeps making up juvenile excuses, like, "I'm too young to think about commitment," "Let's wait until junior high," or, "Ms. Medford, you're my teacher!" Am I crazy to invest so much time in someone so immature?

A. All men are immature. The good news is you've gotten a hold of your dream guy early and can break him of any bad habits before they've taken root. After all, as your student, he's already used to doing what you tell him. So tell him to get with the program! And since studies show that women outlive men, your age difference should guarantee you'll spend more golden years together. I give this relationship an A+!

Q. I really like my sister's husband (I'll call him "Bob"). He likes me too, I can tell, but he's hiding it. Every time I'm around the two of them, he goes to great lengths to convince me (himself) that he adores my sister. Wrapping his arms around her, kissing her, telling her he loves her. <u>Eww</u>! Sometimes I just want to scream, "Stop the charade! You don't have to pretend with me!" I don't want to hurt my sister, but what do I do? Help!

A. You're very astute to pick up on his pathetic attempts to put a Band-aid on a crumbling marriage. I know you don't want to hurt your sister, but isn't it far more cruel to let her (and Bob) go on living a lie? So, as with any band-age, removing it slowly only prolongs the pain. Rip him out of her arms before she has time to say "ouch!", and your love will be like hydrogen peroxide, healing the wound of all that wasted time.

It's All in How You Look at Things

- ♥ You're not desperate, you're enthusiastic.

- ♥ You're not pushy, you're determined.

- ♥ You're not obsessing over him, you're goal-oriented.

- ♥ You're not clingy, you're caring.

- ♥ You're not making harassing phone calls, you're thoughtfully checking in on him.

- ♥ You're not a stalker, you're there when he needs you.

Shoot for the Stars

You're Not a Stalker if He Loves You Back

Sure, a celebrity's life looks glamorous, what with the lavish homes, the fancy cars, the multimillion dollar paychecks, and the throngs of admirers. But deep down, under that glitz and glamour, they're just frightened and lonely and desperately looking for "the one." The one who will look beyond their fame and fortune and love them for themselves. And it's up to you let them know that that special someone is waiting for them, right outside in their bushes.

Q. A major movie star is in love with me. I don't want to tell you who. Okay, it's George Clooney. I went to a movie premiere and got him to sign an autograph for me. He wrote, "Best Wishes, George." Not "George Clooney", but "George". Like we're on a first name basis (even though he never asked my name). When I said thank you, he said, "My pleasure." My heart just about stopped! I think he felt the same connection, but couldn't do anything with all the cameras around. Do you think this is for real, or am I just fooling myself?

A. He wrote, "Best Wishes." Not just good wishes, but the best. He wouldn't write that to just anybody. You obviously made an impression on him, and it's clear he "wishes" to see you again. And you need to RSVP "yes" to that invitation. Go to his home (those maps of celebrity homes are more accurate than you think). Hide in the closet, and when he comes home, jump out and yell, "Hey, remember me? I'm the best wishes girl!" Then, when he admits that you're all he's been thinking about, it'll be "Good Night, and Good Luck!"

How to Get into a Celebrity's House

- ❤ Pose as a caterer.

- ❤ Pose as a gardener.

- ❤ Pose as a prostitute (Charlie Sheen only).

- ❤ Fake injury/heart attack outside house.

- ❤ Get "accidentally" clipped by his limo.

- ❤ Valet park celebrity's car, copy house key.

- ❤ Collect for bleeding-heart liberal charity.

- ❤ Dress as Santa, go down chimney (best at Christmas).

Q. I was at my favorite country music star's concert recently in San Diego (and San Francisco, Atlanta, Detroit, Dallas, Boston, New York, Cleveland, Des Moines, Seattle, Memphis . . .) He sings this one song, "I Loved You Before We Met," which is so about me (I've never met him). There's even a line in it that describes me perfectly: "I always knew your love was true, when I stared into your deep blue eyes." And even though my eyes are brown, I think he's not using the real color because that would be too obvious. He's got so many female fans, he doesn't want to let them know about me. I thought that keeping our love secret was okay with me too, but lately (around Detroit), I started to want more. Am I wrong to feel this way? I don't want to hurt his career.

A. You're worried about his career? What about his heart? I'm sure you saw *Walk the Line?* It didn't hurt Johnny Cash one bit when he asked June Carter to be his bride. You two can make beautiful music together. And before you know it, you'll have a "Ring of Fire." Around your wedding finger!

Best Places to Meet Celebrities

67% Rehab
8% Movie Premiere
7% Trendy L.A. eatery
4% Trendy N.Y. club
3% Film set
11% Famine-ridden nation (pack a sandwich)

Useful Tip

Drive around Beverly Hills, Malibu, Nashville, etc., until you spot a celebrity. Lightly tap his bumper with yours, forcing him to pull over. It's only a short step from exchanging insurance information to exchanging wedding vows!

● ●

Q. I really like this celebrity, he's a famous talk show host. I've written him a bunch of letters and dropped off some gifts outside his house (gated). I know he really liked the gifts because I've gone through his trash a million times and they weren't in there. But then I get this visit from his "people," telling me to stay away from his house, stop leaving him notes, I'm scaring him, etc. What do you think I should do?

● ●

A. I'll tell you who's scared: his "people." They know that when you two run off together, their jobs will be over. They probably haven't even been giving him your letters. You need to make sure he gets your messages directly. Lipstick on his mirror in the morning will leave an indelible impression and let him know you cared enough to make the extra effort. In no time at all, you'll land yourself that gig as his permanent co-host.

Success Story!

I TOOK YOUR ADVICE AND PARACHUTED INTO THE COMPOUND OF MY FAVORITE FOOTBALL STAR. UNFORTUNATELY HE WAS OUT OF TOWN AND MY LANDING WAS A LITTLE HARDER THAN I'D ANTICIPATED. (I'M IN A WHEELCHAIR NOW AND CAN ONLY MOVE BY BLOWING INTO A STRAW).

BUT GOOD NEWS! I'VE QUALIFIED FOR THE MAKE-A-WISH PROGRAM, AND GUESS WHO'S GETTING A PRIVATE MEETING WITH THE MAN OF HER DREAMS NEXT WEEK?!

Perseverance Pays Off

Never Say Die... Unless You Mean It

In the words of the great statesman Winston Churchill, "Never give in. Never give in. Never, never, never." Okay, sure, he was talking about a world war. But make no mistake, when there's an obstacle between you and the one you love, that is war. And you need to fight until victory is yours. And like the flag that was raised at Iwo Jima, you will proudly raise your ring finger, now encircled in diamonds, and exclaim, "Veni, vidi, vici!" I came, I saw, I conquered!

Q. A guy who broke up with me years ago because he said he never wanted to get married, now claims he's married with two kids and would appreciate me not calling him. I didn't believe him, so I went to his house. I saw a woman and two kids eating dinner with him. (Enclosed please find the photos.) I still care about him. What should I do?

A. Here's your answer in three words: "Sister. Niece. Nephew."

If he'd wanted to get married, he would have married you. He clearly wants to get back together and is trying to make you jealous. Even in the worst-case scenario, if he did foolishly marry someone else, it was probably on the rebound. And those children appear to be at least six or seven years old. Ever hear of something called the "seven-year itch"?

I bet he's desperate to get out of there, or he wouldn't be so worried about you calling and tempting him. Don't give up. Call, write, visit. It's the surest way to turn a "don't" into an "I do!"

P.S. The forced smiles on his "family's" faces repulse me.

Useful Tip

Alcohol does two things: It eliminates fear and brings your true feelings to the surface. So make sure to have a few drinks before picking up the phone.

Success Story!

- -

Even when someone's married, that's no reason to give up on him. I took your advice, and although my guy didn't scare easily, his wife sure did! Well, you know what they say, "If you can't stand the heat, get out of the flame-engulfed house." And with her out of the picture, he came running (well, limping) back to me.

Q. I've just gotten out of jail after serving time for the "stalking" and false imprisonment of my ex-boyfriend. Should I give up on him?

A. Give up? That's not how Donald Trump made it. Please fill in the following: "If at first you don't succeed . . ." And besides, who defines "false imprisonment"? A few lousy weeks chained in your basement doesn't exactly make him Nelson Mandela. I don't hear you whining about your time behind bars. But happily, "Absence makes the heart grow fonder." So if you're just getting out of jail, he should be so hot for you right now!

Places to Hide So You Can Keep Tabs on Your Man

- Behind some bushes.

- In your car.

- Up a neighbor's tree.

- In his closet.

- In the heating ducts
  (good because you can go from room to room).

More Motivational Films

- ❤ *Fatal Attraction*

- ❤ *Boxing Helena*

- ❤ *Wicker Park*

- ❤ *Single White Female*

- ❤ *Misery*

Q. There's this guy I really like, and I know he likes me too. Although I think he's afraid to tell me because he's marrying someone else next week. Do you think it's too late for me?

● ●

A. Too late for true love? I don't think so. Didn't you ever see *The Graduate?* Or *Four Weddings and a Funeral?* Or *Wedding Crashers?* A wedding can be the perfect place to let him know how you feel. They even ask, "Does anyone here know any reason why these two should not be wed?" You owe it to both of you to run down that aisle screaming, "I do! I do!" Then, after you've declared your love (and booted everyone out of the front two rows of the bride's section and replaced them with your family), you'll be ready to say, "I do, I do" all over again.

● ●

Still More Motivational Films

- ❤ The Graduate
- ❤ Four Weddings and a Funeral
- ❤ Wedding Crashers

Success Story!

I took your advice and it worked! Tom and I have never been happier. In fact he's now living with me (soundproof basement). He says "I love you" every day. Or he doesn't eat.

Q. This guy told me he's just not that into me. Do you think that means he's not into me?

A. Everyone knows that men are afraid of their feelings, so of course he's not going to share his true feelings with you. Hence his convenient cover-up. There have been numerous books written about the lengths that men will go to avoid telling you that they're not that into you. The fact that he's telling you he's not that into you means only one thing: He is *soooo* into you.

A Final Word

Think how great it feels to be in a relationship. It's exciting, invigorating, you're floating on air! The world is yours, you can accomplish anything! You deserve those feelings, whether or not the man of your dreams is resistant to giving them to you. Numerous studies have shown that the most effective way to achieve something is to act as if you already have it. Act as if you're already in the perfect relationship, already committed, and soon you will be. By applying the lessons learned in this book, you will be able to take the seemingly unattainable, attain it, and lock it up tight so that it never gets away.

About The Author

Danielle Whitman is a popular columnist and the author of numerous books on love and relationships, including, *The Girls' Guide to Hunting and Catching; Ready! Aim! Desire!* and *From Leaving You To Loving You—You Hold The Key.* Although never married, Danielle is seldom without a man in her life.